NOR...

A pocke...

BY CLIV...

CONTENTS

Situated at the top of that distinctive bulge on the eastern side of England, Norfolk is one of those places that you can't really visit on the way to somewhere else. Perhaps it's above all the legacy of this comparative isolation which has given Norfolk its special character.

Of course, the popular misconception is that Norfolk is flat. True, there are flat places – the Broadland marshes close to the coast, and the wide flat plains of the Fens, but much of Norfolk is in fact pleasantly rolling countryside.

A county rich in history, it was once the centre of the weaving industry, the wealth from which produced a number of impressive churches. And although much of the land is farmed, there are also many places of great natural beauty.

Norwich

The ancient and beautiful cathedral city of Norwich still manages to preserve its unique and fascinating character, despite the inevitable modern developments. The Romans settled nearby at Caistor St Edmund way back in AD 70, and the city itself started in Saxon times, developing in a loop in the River Wensum – the name Wensum is Saxon for winding. Apart from providing communication with the sea, the river also provided a natural defence, which was augmented by the flint barrier of the city wall, still visible in many places.

Over a hundred years ago, the writer George Borrow wrote that 'Norwich is a fine old city.' The sentiment is still echoed on the signs on every major road leading into it. Norwich contains more than the average number of medieval churches, and a fair smattering of interesting pubs! It used to be said that there was a church for every week of the year, and a pub for every day, but development has put paid to some of that.

Right: *the city wall still survives in several places; this section can be seen near Silver Road*
Far right: *Bishop's Bridge, the oldest medieval bridge in Norwich. Alongside is the Lollards' Pit, where heretics were burnt*
Below: *the Riverside Walk, Norwich*
Below right: *Cow Tower*

The castle, prominent on its grassy mound, was built in the twelfth century, replacing a wooden one erected on the same spot by the Normans just after the invasion. Although it was quite obviously built to be defended, its military importance waned in the fourteenth century when the city wall was built, and indeed, the only real military excitement was the short episode during Henry III's reign when it fell into the hands of the French. It was reoccupied by the English after King Louis was defeated at Lincoln.

The castle spent much of its life serving as the county gaol, and the keep was refaced with Bath stone in 1834, which accounts for its pristine appearance. Now, it houses a museum which includes the world-famous collection of paintings by members of the 'Norwich School', artists such as Crome, Cotman, Stannard, Thirtle and Ladbrooke – all inspired by the Dutch landscape painters. The castle battlements provide a good view out over the city. The adjacent old cattle market, currently in use as a car park, will be given time to yield its archaeological treasures before a new shopping complex is built.

Norwich Market nearby, one of the largest permanent markets in the country borders on Gentleman's Walk, known as 'The Walk', a street which has become just that since it was pedestrianised. Behind the market stands the imposing City Hall, opened in 1938 by King George VI. This stands on the site of Norwich's first bank, which was run by the Gurney family, founders of Barclays Bank. The family is commemorated in a fascinating clock in Chapelfield Gardens – a horological curiosity reputed to be the most complex mechanical clock in the world. To the right, as you face the City Hall, is the lovely 600-year-old flint Guildhall – in its time, a gaol, seat of local government, courthouse, and now Norwich's Tourist Information Centre.

Further along The Walk stands St Peter Mancroft, one of the largest parish churches in England, noted for its fine peal of bells. The famous seventeenth-century writer and physician Sir Thomas Browne is buried here, and a statue of him can be found on nearby Hay Hill.

Above: *St Peter Mancroft, one of the largest parish churches in England*
Right: *Norwich Castle's impressive Norman keep towers over Castle Meadow*
Below: *the City Hall and the Guildhall look out over the brightly coloured tilts of Norwich market-place*

Undoubtedly Norwich's finest landmark is its magnificent Norman cathedral, with its graceful spire, the second highest in the country. Bishop Herbert de Losinga started the building in 1096, ordered to do so by the Pope as penance for buying his Bishopric. The stone was transported by boat from Normandy, and up the river, to be off-loaded at Pull's Ferry, the ancient water-gate to the cathedral. The spire is fifteenth century, and replaced an earlier one which collapsed in 1362.

The cloisters are the biggest in England, and the Cathedral Close itself, with its picturesque collection of medieval houses, once a monastic precinct, is now a quiet refuge from the bustle and traffic of the city. The King Edward VI School is here, too; its most famous pupil was undoubtedly Horatio Nelson. Also to be found in the cathedral grounds is the grave of Nurse Edith Cavell, who was shot by the Germans in Belgium in 1915 for helping allied prisoners to escape. The cobbled area outside the Close, with its two impressive gateways, is Tombland, site of the Saxon market-place. The Ethelbert Gate was built by townsfolk as a penance for damage done to the monastery in a riot in 1272 between monks and townsfolk.

Opposite: *Norwich's graceful Norman cathedral, an inspiring sight from any angle*
Top left: *the peaceful precincts of the Cathedral Close*
Bottom left: *the cathedral cloisters*

The charming cobbled street of Elm Hill is a must for any visitor. It's here that you can recapture the flavour of bygone years as you walk past buildings ranging from Tudor to Georgian, and the atmosphere of early Victorian street lamps created by an award-winning lighting scheme makes this a pleasant stroll at night. Sadly, the elm from which the street derives its name is no longer here, a victim of the plague of Dutch Elm disease which swept the country some years ago. Standing in its place is a more hardy plane tree.

Another shopping street with a flavour of the past is Bridewell Alley, which has medieval origins. Here you'll find the Bridewell Museum, with its displays illustrating local industries and rural crafts, and Colman's Mustard Shop, which also houses a fascinating museum.

The arts are certainly well represented in Norwich. Apart from the Norwich School of painters, there's the Theatre Royal, with a tradition stretching back to 1757. It regularly puts on national productions of theatre, ballet and opera, many of which are 'pre-London', and is one of the few provincial theatres in the country to be a commercial success. And there's the Maddermarket Theatre, probably one of the most famous amateur theatres, with its custom of anonymity amongst its players.

On the outskirts of the city, at the University of East Anglia, stands the award-winning ultra-modern steel architecture of the Sainsbury Centre. It houses Robert Sainsbury's own art collection, along with regular displays of national exhibitions.

Opposite: *stepping back in time on Elm Hill, Norwich*
Below: *the Sainsbury Centre, a space-age building designed by Norman Foster. The windows at each end of the building contain some of the largest sheets of glass in the world*

The Broads

East Anglia was once the most heavily populated area in the country, and lack of timber for fuel led to the establishment of peat diggings on a massive scale. They flooded when the sea level rose during the Middle Ages, forming the reed-fringed lakes we see today. The traditional industry of cutting the reeds is still an essential part of the management which stops the Broads becoming overgrown. Norfolk reed is the finest thatching material available, lasting fifty to sixty years on the roof of a house, compared with just thirty to forty for wheat thatch.

The grazing marshes, of which the largest area is at Halvergate, are perhaps most representative of a Broadland landscape, with lush green fields grazed by cows and intersected by dykes, the skyline broken by the old windpumps which used to keep the land drained. Broadland is the last refuge for the swallowtail butterfly, Britain's largest and rarest butterfly.

The delicate ecology of the Broads, and the system of rivers and dykes which links them, have been under pressure from a variety of threats, including water pollution, erosion to river-banks caused by motor-boats, and intensive farming. The Broads now have National Park status, and the Broads Authority administers the area so as to ensure that

recreation and commercial interests are compatible with the primary interests of conservation.

The 125 miles of navigable waterways have long been popular amongst boating holiday-makers, although much can be seen by taking short walks along the river-banks. You may even be lucky enough to see the huge black sail of the Ludham-based *Albion*, the last surviving trading wherry. The wherries were once common sights on the Broadland waterways.

The Weavers' Way, a 56-mile footpath from Cromer to Great Yarmouth, passes through Broadland, and walking a section of it can make an excellent day out. There are also good circular walks, each taking around $2\frac{1}{2}$ hours, starting at Dilham, Horning, Horsey, Martham, Ludham and Potter Heigham.

Opposite: *Halvergate Marshes – a typical Broads grazing-marsh landscape*, (inset) *swallowtail butterfly*
Top: *Horsey Mill*
Left: *the* Albion, *last of the trading wherries*
Below: *pleasure boats on the River Bure at Horning Ferry*

Wroxham and Horning are popular spots, and a good many boating holidays start here, so they tend to be fairly busy. Most of the Broads are clustered along the Rivers Bure, Ant and Thurne, whilst the River Waveney and the Yare, which carries sea-going vessels all the way to Norwich, link up with the northern Broads rivers by the tidal reaches of Breydon Water.

Apart from a fine view from the top of its tower, St Helen's Church at Ranworth, the 'Cathedral of the Broads', has one of the best examples of a painted rood screen in the country. Nearby, a board-walk nature trail takes you to the Norfolk Naturalists' Trust Broadland Conservation Centre, a thatched building floating on pontoons at the edge of Ranworth Broad. Its displays give an excellent insight into the Broads, and a viewing gallery gives visitors the opportunity to watch some of the wildlife, including herons and the great crested grebe.

Water quality is one of the most important concerns in Broadland – phosphate pollution has combined with nitrates from fertilisers to cloud the water with algae, stifling most water-borne life. One of the Broads Authority's great successes is Cockshoot Broad, near Horning. They dammed it off from the river, and pumped out about three feet of mud. Within three months, seeds at the bottom of the Broad started to shoot, and the water is now clear again.

Top left: *Wroxham Broad*
Top right: *rood screen at Ranworth church*
Bottom: *water-lilies grow in abundance in the cleared waters of Cockshoot Dyke,* (inset) *great crested grebe*

One of the Broads' more unusual sights is on the River Bure. St Benet's Abbey, built in the ninth century, was a vast and wealthy Benedictine monastery until the Dissolution, when most of the buildings were dismantled for their stone. The title of Abbot of St Benet's was transferred to the Bishop of Norwich, who to this day holds a service at the ruins of St Benet's once a year, on the first Sunday in August. A windmill was built into the gatehouse 200 years ago, which accounts for the confused edifice which remains.

The Environmental Centre at How Hill is well worth a visit. Here you can take a trip on an Edwardian-style electric boat. It glides almost silently through the reeds, giving you the best opportunity to see a variety of birds without disturbing them. Here too is the 100-year-old Toad Hole Cottage, a tiny thatched house, once the home of an eel-catcher.

The Nature Reserve at Hickling is one of the best places to see the swallowtail butterfly, from May to July. There's a 'Water Trail', a boat trip which takes you out into the reed and sedge beds, with a stop to let you walk through woodlands. It's well worth the effort of climbing the ladder sixty feet to an observation platform up in an oak tree. The views are commanding, and you may well spot a marsh harrier.

Top left: *St Benet's Abbey – one of the more curious sights on the Broads*
Top right: *Toad Hole Cottage, How Hill*
Bottom: *the peaceful reed-fringed waters of Hickling Broad*

Above all, the Broads are characterised by their distinctive mills. Not all of them were built to grind corn. On the low-lying marshes closer to the coast, they were used as drainage pumps. Sutton Mill, near Stalham, is the tallest tower mill in the country, with nine floors, and a fascinating collection of old machinery and tools.

The southern end of Breydon Water is overlooked by Burgh Castle, where the Roman fort of Gàriannonum was built on what was once a vast estuary. The views from the ruins are spectacular, with Berney Arms Mill on the opposite bank, and Halvergate Marshes beyond.

Nearby is the seaside resort of Great Yarmouth. Once the herring capital of Europe, Yarmouth is still a thriving port, much concerned with North Sea oil, and of course it's a great favourite for traditional family seaside holidays. Anna Sewell, author of the children's classic *Black Beauty,* was born here, and Charles Dickens wrote *David Copperfield* whilst staying at the Royal Hotel in 1843.

Left: *Thurne Dyke Wind-pump, a fully restored example of a Broadland drainage pump*
Below: *Great Yarmouth, a perennial favourite for family holidays by the sea*

North Norfolk

The North Norfolk coast between Hunstanton and Cromer runs for some thirty miles almost exactly west/east. And whilst those towns, along with Cromer's neighbour Sheringham, bustle with holiday-makers in the summer, the commercial side of holidays tails off sharply in between. The countryside differs quite markedly along those thirty miles. In the west, the coastline is a tortuous maze of creeks and inlets in a vast expanse of saltmarsh and mudflat. It's a birdwatchers' paradise, and whatever time of the year you visit, there will always be plenty to see. Further east, the countryside takes on more of a rolling aspect, with steep cliffs rising from the sea.

This strip of coast is rich in nature reserves, with over a dozen, including Cley Marshes, the first of the county naturalists' trust reserves which can now be found all over the country. The North Norfolk coast is also an Area of Outstanding Natural Beauty, with its own long-distance footpath – the Norfolk Coast Path, which runs from just outside Hunstanton to Cromer.

Blakeney Point is a thin spit of land about four miles long, sprouting from the coast just north of Cley. The shingle bank makes walking heavy going, so most tend to take a short boat trip out to the nature reserve, where you won't just see birds and plants, but also have a good chance of spotting seals basking on the sandbanks.

Main picture: *visitors enjoying the wild, sandy landscape of Blakeney Point, owned by the National Trust. This area provides ideal habitats for a wide variety of birds and plants*
Inset left: *Blakeney Quay – a popular mooring for pleasure boats*
Inset right: *common seal*

You could spend an entire holiday nature-watching on the North Norfolk coast, but there are other attractions as well. The general character of the area is underlined by the houses, cottages and churches which are built in the local flint, the prettiest ones with knapped flint walls, in which the round flints have been split in two to expose a flat face of rich dark colour.

Sandringham, a favourite retreat for the Royal Family, was built in 1870 by Edward, Prince of Wales. The house and gardens are open to the public except when members of the Royal Family are in residence. The estate – heath, forest and parkland – has been described as 'a piece of Scotland south of the Tweed'.

Castle Rising, north of King's Lynn, used to be a busy port before the sea receded. The castle's Norman keep, largely intact, stands on earthworks of Roman origin.

Hunstanton caters for those wanting a traditional family seaside holiday. It's the only east coast resort where you can watch the sun set over the sea, and it has some magnificent cliffs, with distinctive bands of colour made from layers of red carr stone and white chalk. Just around the coast, near Holme, you can find some marvellous walking, both out in the dunes, and inland on the chalk downs around Ringstead.

Top: *Sandringham House – a favourite retreat for the Royal Family*
Bottom left: *Holme Dunes Nature Reserve. The Norfolk Coast Path passes close by.*
Photo: Clive Tully
Bottom right: *the Norman keep of Castle Rising*

Nearby, at Heacham, is Caley Mill, the home of Norfolk Lavender Ltd, the largest lavender producers in the country. The plants are a marvellous blaze of colour during the summer, and you can tour the mill to see the various drying and distillation processes.

There are no fewer than six villages with the prefix Burnham, lying between Brancaster and Holkham. Most notable is Burnham Thorpe, birthplace of England's greatest sailor, Horatio Nelson. Although his father's parsonage no longer stands, a plaque beside the road marks the site. The cross and lectern in the church are made from timbers taken from Nelson's ship HMS *Victory*, which was also the source of the flags which hang in the nave.

The Norfolk home of the earls of Leicester, Holkham Hall is a magnificent Palladian mansion set in beautiful parkland. Using some of the ideas of 'Turnip' Townsend, Thomas William Coke turned the estate from what was almost wasteland into an agricultural success.

Holkham Bay is a flat expanse of sand which gives you quite a walk to get to the sea when the tide is out. Fringed with pine trees, it provides a pleasant walk round to the small port of Wells-next-the-Sea.

As you come over the hill on the A140 into Cromer, with your first view of the sea, you can't fail to notice the magnificent church tower, the tallest in Norfolk. The climb up the steps to the top is well worth it for the view. Cromer is known far and wide for its crabs, and for the most famous lifeboatman of them all, Henry Blogg.

Above: *Caley Mill, at Heacham, the home of Norfolk lavender.* Photo: GGS Photography, copyright Norfolk Lavender Ltd

Top right: *Holkham Hall stands in magnificent grounds landscaped by Capability Brown*

Centre right: *fishing boats on the beach at Cromer, a traditional seaside resort on the North Norfolk coast*

Below: *pine woods fringe the bay at Holkham*

Top left: *the beach at Sheringham*
Top right: *Felbrigg Hall*
Bottom left: *one of the great houses of Norfolk – Blickling Hall*
Centre right: *the shrine at Walsingham*
Bottom right: *keeping the age of steam alive on the North Norfolk Railway.* Photo: Brian Fisher

Nearby seventeenth-century Felbrigg Hall is a National Trust property, worth visiting, and at Sheringham you can find the old railway station, which still runs steam trains along the coast to Weybourne and has recently been extended inland to Holt. There's another steam railway further along the coast, the Wells and Walsingham Light Railway. Walsingham is famous for its shrine, which has been a place of pilgrimage for hundreds of years.

Just outside the market town of Aylsham is Blickling Hall, a magnificent Jacobean building of red brick standing on the site of an earlier house which was the family home of Anne Boleyn. The long gallery has a superb plasterwork ceiling, and the grounds themselves are glorious. One of the outbuildings contains the Hawk Trust's National Centre for Owl Conservation, with a fascinating exhibition about barn owls and the threats to their habitats.

The small village of Worstead near North Walsham was once at the heart of the weaving industry. Until the fourteenth century, English wool was exported to the Continent as raw material, and very little was woven here. When he married Philippa of Hainault in 1326, Edward III banned the import of foreign cloth, enticing enterprising Flemish weavers to settle in East Anglia. Sixteenth-century Dutch weavers fleeing from the Spanish brought with them the technique of combing the wool rather than carding it, which produced a longer staple. Although the practice originated in Lombardy, the resulting cloth became known here as worsted, after the village where it started in England.

South and West of Norwich

East Dereham is the birthplace of the author George Borrow. The infamous Bishop Bonner was rector of St Nicholas's Church in the 1530s, living in the nearby thatched cottage with ornamental plasterwork. During Mary Tudor's reign he earned the name 'Bloody Bonner' for sending Protestants to be burned at the stake.

In the churchyard can be found the grave of the melancholic poet William Cowper, and St Withburga's Well, the site of the grave of one of the Saxon King Anna's sainted daughters. Miracles are said to have taken place here. The saint's body was spirited away by the abbot of Ely, and the desecrated grave erupted with the spring now known as St Withburga's Well.

Hingham's fine church reflects the local wealth of the period when weaving was at its height. But many weavers fleeing religious persecution emigrated to America during the seventeenth century. Samuel Lincoln founded Hingham, Massachusetts, and one of his descendants, Abraham, became President.

Despite considerable housing and industrial development, the market town of Wymondham still has great charm, typified perhaps by its octagonal wooden market cross. Wymondham Abbey is a strange mixture of Norman church with fifteenth-century towers, and is surrounded by various remains of the former priory. The twin towers came about when the Pope ordered the segregation of the church in the thirteenth century, after quarrels between the townsfolk and the Benedictine monks.

Wymondham was the place where Kett's Rebellion began in 1549, when peasants led by Robert Kett revolted against landowners enclosing common land. The rebels overran Norwich, and controlled much of Norfolk before being put down by an army of 12,000 men under the Earl of Warwick. Kett was hanged at Norwich Castle, his brother William from one of the towers of Wymondham Abbey.

The original town of Diss, in the Waveney Valley, along which the southern boundary of Norfolk runs, was built around the Mere, a six-acre lake. John Skelton, a past rector of St Mary's Church, was Poet Laureate, and tutor to the young Henry VIII.

Not far from Diss are Bressingham Gardens, with lavish displays of hardy perennials and alpine plants in a parkland setting. Here too is Bressingham Live Steam Museum, with a fine collection of working engines.

To the east of Diss is Scole, with its fine red-brick coaching inn, and further on, Billingford Windmill, a fully restored corn mill with five-storey red-brick tower, and a boat-shaped cap.

Near Bungay, at Earsham, the Otter Trust continues its successful breeding programme for the British otter, reintroducing animals to the wild wherever suitable habitats remain.

Opposite: *Diss Mere*
Top left: *Wymondham's octagonal wooden Market Cross*
Centre left: *Billingford windmill*
Bottom left: *colourful pargeting and a thatched roof add character to Bishop Bonner's Cottage, East Dereham*

Breckland and the Fens

Mainly as a result of drainage and reclamation in the seventeenth century, Fenland, once a wasteland of marshes, is now the country's most productive agricultural region. Most of the important work was carried out by the Dutch engineer Cornelius Vermuyden, whose drainage channels short-cut the winding Fenland rivers.

Apart from making the surrounding countryside fit for year-round agriculture, the drainage regime has turned the Ouse Washes, an area between two parallel drainage cuts, into an important wildlife habitat.

Black-tailed godwits, once rarely seen in Britain, now breed here regularly along with snipe, mallard, coots, reed warblers and many other birds. Winter flooding tends to vary in depth from several feet to a few inches, providing a wide range of waterfowl habitats. The Ouse Washes are a particularly important habitat for roughly half the British population of Bewick's swans.

Situated at the outfall of a number of interconnected rivers, the ancient town of King's Lynn serviced the trading needs of a huge inland area. Today, it's still a thriving port and industrial centre. The Guildhall of St George is England's largest example of a medieval merchant's house. It is now used as a theatre, as indeed it was in an earlier period, when Shakespeare himself appeared on stage there. The Trinity Guildhall houses the town's treasures, including the King

John Cup and Sword, which date back to the time of the Royal Charter awarded by King John.

The light sandy soils of Breckland once supported vast forests, but Neolithic man cleared them to grow his crops. In time, and further weakened by over-grazing, the area became unable to support any more growth. The present afforestation, the second largest in the country, was planted in 1922 in what was virtually a desert!

Above: *Tuesday Market, King's Lynn.*
The market here was established in the
twelfth century
Left: *the Peddars Way starts in Breckland,*
flanked by woodland and open fields
Below: *one of the most famous of King's Lynn's*
many historic buildings is the Customs House,
which dates from the seventeenth century

Norfolk's own National Trail, the Peddars Way, runs through here, following the line of a pre-Roman route – indeed, much of the path is an ancient monument! Whether walked in sections, or perhaps over several days for a holiday, the Peddars Way from Knettishall to Holme-next-the-Sea, and the Norfolk Coast Path around to Cromer, offer the finest variety of landscapes of any of the major long-distance paths.

The water levels in the Breckland meres, such as Lang Mere and Ring Mere in East Wretham Heath Nature Reserve, seem to have minds of their own, rising and falling, even disappearing altogether, without any apparent connection with the weather. The determining factor is the water table in the underlying chalk.

The red-brick manor of Oxburgh Hall has the largest fifteenth-century gatehouse in existence. Mary Queen of Scots was imprisoned here, and the needlework with which she whiled away her time is still here – the Oxburgh Hangings. Nearby is Cockley Cley, where an Iceni camp has been reconstructed on its original site.

Not graves at all, but a vast collection of diggings where flint was mined, Grimes Graves is the most important prehistoric site in Norfolk. Here, men dug down through the chalk, tunnelling in dreadful conditions. One of the shafts is open to the public.

Top left: *Scots pines at East Wretham*
Top right: *Oxburgh Hall, a moated manor house which has been the home of the Bedingfield family for nearly 500 years*
Bottom: *the reconstructed Iceni camp at Cockley Cley*

Once the most important cathedral city in East Anglia, Thetford still has extensive remains of its priory, which are worth visiting. Local flint abounds, and the Ancient House Museum has displays about flint-knapping – the shaping of tiny flints for use in firearms. The statue of Thomas Paine commemorates Thetford's most famous son, the campaigner for human rights, who influenced both the American and French Revolutions.

According to local folklore, the lavishly appointed church in the market town of Swaffham was paid for by John Chapman, the Pedlar of Swaffham. He met a stranger in London who described having dreamt of finding a treasure in the pedlar's garden. The pedlar returned home to find everything just as he had been told, and celebrated his new-found wealth by building the north aisle of the church.

Below: *the River Thet at Thetford,* (inset) *remains of the twelfth-century Cluniac priory at Thetford*